Ginger
A Spice for Life

BY DAVID ROSER

PLANTSCAN PUBLICATIONS

Published by:

Plantscan Publications
PO Box 40
Bury St Edmunds
Suffolk IP31 2SS

Printed and bound by Cavendish Press, Leicester, England

ISBN number 0 - 9529479 - 0 - 0

Plantscan Publications is a division of Plantscan Development.

GINGER

Ginger

Zingiber Officinalis

Originating from Tropical Asia, this medicinal herb with its warming

properties has been used in the West now for over 2000 years.

In cooking, ginger can be added to a variety of dishes & people throughout

the world are continuing to enjoy the aromatic flavour of this spice.

CONTENTS

FOREWORD

I first became interested in ginger whilst researching my original book on garlic and noticed at that time how similar in some ways the activities of ginger and garlic appeared to be especially in their common ability to tackle some of the parameters associated with cardio-vascular disease.

Interest, however, moved on to become a more consuming desire to know more and the further and deeper you look, the more you find. In the case of ginger, a whole new area of researches carried out over the last ten years in universities and hospitals across the world paid testament to ginger as a potentially serious medicinal material.

As with garlic, ginger is believed to be completely safe when used with discretion. It also happens to taste good, and as you will see with ginger tea, can also make you feel good too! But what is so satisfying is the wide range of health problems which ginger can tackle. As with garlic this is no doubt due to the large number of individual components which make up ginger's chemistry, many of which can be singularly identified as active in the body.

Finally, I would like to thank Dr. Stephen Fulder and Dr. Meir Tenne for their support and unstinted encouragement in pursuing ginger to its roots! But my most grateful thanks go to Joanna Pope for her hard and valiant work in ensuring that this book has gone successfully to press.

DAVID ROSER

THE $\mathscr{H}$ISTORY OF GINGER

The use of ginger as a food ingredient and for its perceived medicinal actions stretches right back into the mists of time. Its exact origins are unknown but it is native to the tropical jungles of South-East Asia and is understood to have been cultivated there for over 3000 years. In traditional Chinese, Ayurvedic and Graeco-Arabic (otherwise known as Tibb) system of medicine, ginger has been used for thousands of years to treat various ailments.

History is peppered with references to this pungent aromatic spice.

History is peppered with references to this pungent aromatic spice and it is fascinating to follow its use via an often dramatic path up to its increasing popularity in the present day. Now, it is widely available at a reasonable cost, making it easily obtainable for anyone who learns to appreciate its value as an ingredient in many dishes, both savoury and sweet, primarily for its distinctive piquant flavour. Its long-revered stomach-soothing effects come as a welcome extra.

However, it was not always so as we shall see, with the astonishing importance of the spice trade in general through history giving such items an extremely high value which extended well past Tudor times.

Chinese medical books written more than 2000 years ago mention the use of ginger.

Chinese medical books written more than 2000 years ago mention the use of ginger and, to this day, it forms an integral part of a great percentage of prescriptions for ailments. It was also used in the Middle East and Southern parts of Europe well before the days of the Roman Empire which lasted from 27BC, when Octavian became emperor as Augustus, to 476AD.

By this time spices generally had assumed such importance that, in 24BC, attempts by the Emperor Augustus to reduce their ludicrously high prices were recorded as he tried to incorporate the South Arabian spice kingdom into the Roman Empire, a project doomed to failure. And, a little over a hundred years later, Christian prophet John of Ephesus was moved to announce that the use of spices was one of the excesses that would bring about the fall of Rome.

At this point one might be forgiven for wondering just what the tremendous importance of the addition of such apparently insignificant items to the diet could be and how they reached such astronomic value.

Although we have no way of knowing exactly when spices and herbs were first used as part of a meal, it would seem likely - as they originate in the warmer areas of the word - that they had been found to delay food items such as meat and fish going bad, as well as covering up "off" flavours.

Rancidity of the fatty parts of foods is a particular problem and using spices and herbs in meal preparation can delay this happening possibly because several spices, including ginger, are now known to contain antioxidants, as well as being an antibacterial agent.

Even in more temperate climates, ways of keeping food fresh and palatable were few (mainly consisting of wine vinegars and salt petre) and of especial importance where people, often the richer ones, tended to eat a lot of meat, as in Europe. Thus spices became valuable trading tools and, being mainly grown on islands almost half way round the world, had great distances to travel from market to market. The growers sold them to traders who transported them to the coast where they changed hands many times before being taken up the Red Sea to Egypt. From there the precious cargoes went overland by camel train to the Mediterranean, ships took them to Venice in Italy, from where they were sold all over Europe.

Precious cargoes went overland by camel train, ships took them to Venice in Italy, from where they were sold all over Europe.

So transport was slow and costly, and goods changed hands many times in transit to the final destination, and consequently their cost and importance rocketed.

Should the value of spices down the ages be doubted here are just two examples of the esteem in which they were held. When he sacked ancient Rome in 410AD, Alaric the Goth came across a storehouse containing

2265kg (5000lb) of pepper and, in the 14th century in England, one pound of ginger was equated to the value of a sheep!

It was in 201AD that Arab and Persian sailors reached the Spice Islands for the first time and Arab merchants reportedly introduced Oriental spices to the Mediterranean, and some time after that - in 901AD - England saw her first shipment of East Indian spices. They were also brought back to England by Christians returning from the Crusades. At that time, they were used mainly for their reputed medical benefits and usually only to flavour food by those who could well afford the high prices.

However, worse was to come, for prices rose dramatically around 1453 when the Turks captured Constantinople, conquered Egypt, and blocked the movement of spices. Previously a treasure well worth seeking, the lust for a source of spices - especially pepper, ginger, cinnamon, cloves, nutmeg and mace - now truly triggered a spate of daring exploration and conquest as men of more adventurous spirit, and perhaps greed, started to consider whether there could possibly be another route to the Spice Islands which wouldn't involve travelling through Turkish-held lands.

The lust for a source of spices - especially pepper, ginger, cinnamon, cloves, nutmeg and mace - now truly triggered a spate of daring exploration and conquest.

Remembering at this time that most people were still of the opinion that the world was flat and that you would fall over the edge if you sailed too far, Christopher Columbus's conviction that it was actually round and that he could therefore sail to the Spice Islands by going westwards instead of travelling east must have seemed suicidal at the very least.

Nonetheless, he set sail in 1492, arriving at a likely group of islands, he believed, after some weeks at sea. It was only after his death that people began to realise that he had, in fact, discovered the archipelago which extends from the Florida peninsula in North America to the coast of Venezuela, naming it the West Indies in the belief that he had found the west route to South East Asia and India.

In 1522, the Portuguese explorer Ferdinand Magellan actually reached the East Indies, but was killed in a skirmish with natives of islands later called the Philippines. His lieutenant, del Cano, returned to Seville with the surviving crew and a cargo of cloves, the value of which more than covered the cost of the expedition which had completed the first circumnavigation of the globe. Accompanying this voyage was an Italian scholar, Antonia Plgafetta who noted that, in several places, green ginger was eaten in the same ways as bread.

In 1561, English navigator John Hawkins captured a Portuguese ship carrying African slaves to Brazil and traded hundreds of them for ginger, pearls and sugar at a tremendous profit. Rather than try to break Portugal's monopoly on the spice trade at this time, the English found it was easier to hijack Portuguese ships, it seems.

In 1561, English navigator John Hawkins captured a Portuguese ship carrying African slaves to Brazil and traded hundreds of them for ginger.

Jamaican ginger arrived in Europe on a ship from the West Indies in 1585 - the first Oriental spice to be grown successfully in the New World.

Then in 1594 Lisbon closed the spice market to the English and Dutch, triggering the founding of the Dutch East India Company in order to obtain spices direct. The Dutch has established control of the spice trade by 1599, raising prices dramatically, thereby forcing the English to form their own East India company.

Under the command of James Lancaster, the first English spice fleet sailed from Woolwich in 1601, returning eventually with a cargo including a million pounds (lbs) of pepper.

Queen Elizabeth I was a noted fan and even employed her own full-time gingerbread baker in the late 16th century.

Prior to this, ginger was already popular in England, both as a medicinal and culinary spice - in fact, next to pepper it was the most sough-after flavouring. It was known in England before the Norman Conquest, Chaucer mentioned its use, and Henry VIII famously ordered it to be employed as a plague preventative but it is not known where he got this idea from or whether it was effective. It was included in pomanders and potpourris used at the time to disguise foul odours, and gingerbread was widely sold as a treat throughout the country. Queen Elizabeth I was a noted fan and even employed her own full-time gingerbread baker in the late 16th century, we are told.

Shakespeare mentioned ginger in the Winter's Tale and Twelfth Night and it was included in a number of recipes, including one for gingerbread in a cookery book written at the time. Gingerbread was originally more a block of honey baked with flour, ginger and spices which was often used as a gift in medieval times. Cloves and box leaves were dipped in gold paint and used as decoration and this gilding of gingerbread went on until the late 19th century in England.

For hundreds of years customers of taverns could help themselves from a jar of ginger kept on ale house counters.

Ginger was also used in England to add a spicy flavour to beer or porter and for hundreds of years customers of taverns could help themselves from a jar of ginger kept on ale house counters. Other readymade products incorporating ginger gradually became popular over the years, including carbonated ginger ale, which first made its appearance in a New York coffee house in the early 1800c, and remain an accepted part of the diet to this very day.

Nowadays, ginger is widely used in recipes in many countries and easily obtained at a reasonable cost. It is commercially grown in Africa, the West Indies, Australia, and South America, with India being the world's largest producer, so we no longer have any fear of being deprived of it's delightful and comforting flavour and effect.

CHAPTER 2

G I N G E R
A S   A   T R A D I T I O N A L
M E D I C I N E

From earliest times, plants have been used as medicines in every part of the world. And, still, a great percentage of the planet's population relies on plant medicine to treat a vast range of ailments.

Nowadays, it is reassuring and comforting to find that modern scientific research has confirmed, and is still confirming, the accuracy of such ancient beliefs which have been passed down through thousands of years. The fascinating thought is how these beliefs came about in the first place. Trial and error and observation of effect over a length of time is obvious in the number of instances where results of ingesting or applying plants and parts of plants to ailments and injuries can be seen fairly rapidly. However, what about more gentle effects, where beneficial results can take months to be apparent? One could be forgiven for wondering how it was worked out which remedies had been responsible for what cures or improvements to health

A great percentage of the planets' population relies on plant medicine to treat a vast range of ailments.

Somewhere very early on, ginger may have crossed the line from being purely a flavouring to being revered as a medicinal substance.

The use of plants and parts of plants which were good to eat and made useful additions as flavourings for other foodstuffs are easier to understand, too, than unpalatable - even slightly poisonous in larger quantities - items. Why were people tempted to use them in the first place? Clues are thought to lie in the instincts of animals still observable today where, when they are feeling under the weather, they will go off and seek certain plants and eat small quantities. Perhaps humans, too, had long-forgotten instincts which led them to certain plants.

Even more strangely, quite independently, tribes and civilisations in different parts of the world learnt to use plants from similar families to give relief from similar ailments and injuries.

In the case of ginger, with its pungent and spicy rhizomes - commonly, although incorrectly, referred to as roots - its increasing popularity as a food flavouring and medicine from earliest recorded times, and no doubt before, could quite easily hail from a liking for its tantalising taste. With its addition to more and more meals, its calming influence on the stomach when it accompanied indigestible or slightly "off" meat and fish in particular, plus its warming action in cold weather, and its toning and enlivening effect generally, must have been noted fairly swiftly, and there have been many hundreds of thousands of grateful users ever since!

So, somewhere very early on, ginger may have crossed the line from being purely a flavouring to being revered as a medicinal substance, too. And, curiously, not so long ago - especially in Britain - it started to revert to being thought of more of an essential ingredient in cakes, biscuits and drinks with little consideration by the modern generation for its traditionally-respected medicinal benefits. Now that is starting to change again as research confirms its age-old applications for improved health.

The many benefits of ginger crop up repeatedly in the historical records of various civilisations. As far back as almost 3000 years before Christ, the legendary Chinese Emperor Shen Mung is credited with the production of a very famous herbal in which the use of ginger is mentioned, as it is in very many ancient Chinese herbals, with a particular appreciation of its ability to remedy the effects of eating too much rich food, or over-indulgence in alcohol. Confucius, the Chinese philosopher who lived from about 551BC to 479BC, was said to keep a side dish of ginger beside him when he ate.

Confucius was said to keep a side dish of ginger beside him when he ate.

To this day, it is used in a vast number of Chinese prescriptions, either for its own benefits or to improve or tone down the potentially somewhat violent effects of other herbs, especially on the digestive system.

The Ayurvedic and Tibb systems of medicine have been known to make use of ginger for thousands of years, too, regarding ginger as a sort of universal medicine, but particularly favouring it for its anti-inflammatory action on musculo-skeletal diseases. Ayurvedic doctors also used ginger for digestive and respiratory problems, and applied it externally as a pain-soother.

De Materia Medica was compiled around 77AD and described nearly 600 plants with their medicinal properties, including ginger.

The Greeks and Romans had a fondness for ginger medicinally as well as in cookery. In fact, ginger was known to be an important ingredient of the Mithridaetus which was a concoction used to protect against poisoning formulated by the physicians of King Mithridates VI around 80BC to help him develop immunity to such threats to his life.

Dioscorides, a Greek physician who is credited with compiling the first pharmacopoeia, travelled extensively in his occupation as surgeon in the Roman Army. His herbal, *De Materia Medica*, was compiled around 77AD and described nearly 600 plants with their medicinal properties, including ginger which he believed to be very useful for the digestion and in helping to relax the stomach.

Indeed, although it was a very expensive item even then, Roman doctors were known to make a point of including ginger as one of the few essential herbal medicines selected to take with them when they accompanied the Roman legions on their travels, especially through colder and damper climates than they were used to. It was regarded as most helpful in warding off chills, and generally keeping the soldiers fit.

Renowned Greek philosopher and religious leader, Pythagoras, who lived in the 6th century BC, founded an ascetic religious order at Crotone in Southern Italy, the rules of which included silence and vegetarianism. He suggested using ginger for its digestive properties, and carminative action - in other words, it helped to expel gas from the stomach and intestines.

GINGER AS A TRADITIONAL MEDICINE

Another famous Greek who was impressed by ginger's heating properties, saying that it produced a more lasting but gentler heat than pepper, was Galen, who lived from about 129 to 199AD, and was a Greek physician and scholar who compiled Greek medical knowledge into treaties which formed the basis of European medicine until the Renaissance.

And in the *Arabian Nights*, sometimes called the *Thousand and One Nights*, a collection of oriental stories of love and adventure dating from the 10th century AD, ginger is mentioned as an aphrodisiac.

In the late Middle Ages, when the Arabs mainly supplied spices to Europe, ginger was often to be found in their own medicine chests. In *The Medicine of the Prophet* written by Al Suyati of Cairo in the late 15th Century, ginger's heating effects were mentioned and the fact that it prevented an excess of damp, soothed the stomach, aided digestion, dissolved wind, acted as an aphrodisiac, and was a help with respiratory problems, so no wonder it was regarded as an important travelling companion!

In the Arabian Nights ginger is mentioned as an aphrodisiac.

Both King Henry VIII and his daughter Queen Elizabeth I are known to have been keen herbalists. Henry ordered ginger to be used as a plague preventative presumably because of the commonly-held belief in its antiseptic qualities at the time, and Elizabeth had made-up a powder to be taken before eating meat to help expel wind, comfort the stomach and help digestion, which consisted mostly of white ginger with cinnamon, caraway, anise and fennel - something which a modern herbalist would have little quarrel with.

John Gerard's famous *Herball*, first published in 1597, mentions ginger's heating and digestive qualities and declared it to be "profitable for the stomacke", while in 1631 John Winthrop the Younger ordered a great number of herbs and medicines, including green ginger, to take on an Atlantic crossing in case he was sick at sea.

In the 17th century, a pungent combination of spices which included ginger and was called Elixir of Vitriol, was the brainchild of a German doctor, Adrian Mynsicht, who proposed it as a remedy for drunkenness.

By the 18th century, however, the passion for ginger was starting to evaporate, at least in recipes, and it tended to be relegated to cakes, puddings and creams. It was, however, mentioned by the Reverend John Wesley in *Primitive Physick* published in 1747, who included a rack of ginger in a remedy for tuberculosis, or consumption, as it was then called.

1631 John Winthrop ordered herbs and medicines including green ginger to take on an Atlantic crossing in case he was sick at sea.

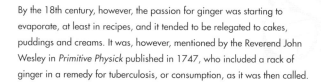

In 1840, ginger was said to be good for wind in *The Family Physician and The Farmer's Companion* which was published in New York, and the advice to avoid heavy suppers and take a remedy which included tincture of ginger was included in *The Family Manual*, also published in New York in 1845. In 1871, it was suggested in the form of lozenges as a remedy for loss of appetite in *The Household Book of Practical Receipts*.

Up until the end of the Second World War, most of the drugs used by doctors were still herbal medicines.

Up until the end of the Second World War, most of the drugs used by doctors were still herbal medicines, and today there is a marked revival of interest in these mostly gentle remedies with their pedigree of problem-free use handed down through thousands of years in several different traditional systems of medicine. Ginger, in particular, is used by modern herbalists for a great many ailments as we shall see - most remedies with their origins in the dim, distant past, but now backed up by the added comfort and vindication of scientific confirmation.

CHAPTER 3

HELPING YOURSELF WITH GINGER

So, what are the ways in which ginger can gently aid the body back to health and wellbeing? According to modern herbalists, these are many, and frequently based on the beliefs and observations handed down the centuries.

Supported by this confidence in its abilities and an almost complete absence of any deleterious side-effects - although large amounts are not recommended for people suffering from skin complaints (it is also a rubefacient, causing reddening of the skin) - ginger certainly continues to earn its place as a supplement or essence in the family medicine cabinet, and a regular food item on the household shopping list.

According to modern herbalists, the beneficial uses of Ginger are frequently based on beliefs and observations handed down the centuries.

Today, it is probably still best-known as a remedy for sickness and vomiting, especially valued by those who suffer from travel sickness, but is also a gentle comfort for women suffering from the miseries of morning sickness.

An ideal companion for the festive season for those prone to over-excitement and over indulgence!

Some regular travellers make a point of taking a flask of ginger tea on journeys for its warming and comforting effect as well as its help in calming feelings of nausea.

Ginger's reputation as a remedy for some of the symptoms of a hangover is no doubt based on its ability to lessen and prevent nausea and to quell an upset stomach - making it an ideal companion for the festive season for those prone to over-excitement and over indulgence!

Ginger has also long been renowned for its ability to soothe digestive upsets, and get rid of flatulence or wind, a frequent curse of those who like rich and fatty foods. Again, as well as taking ginger in capsule or pearls form, it can be drunk as a tea before meals, especially rich and heavy ones, or a little fresh or crystallised ginger can be chewed to improve digestion.

As ginger also activates or encourages the production of saliva, which is, of course, the digestive juice which begins the whole great process of digesting in the mouth, then this is regarded as a very good reason for those who regularly experience digestive problems to try and take ginger in some form before a meal.

And, in an emergency, if you don't happen to have ginger available at the time in capsule or pearls form, then it can be taken in any number of guises - ginger ale or beer, ginger biscuits, you can chew a little crystallised ginger or fresh ginger root, or put a couple of drops of ginger tincture on the tongue. Young children can often be persuaded to eat a ginger snap, even if they won't try anything else.

Ginger is an expectorant, helping to clear airways and lungs of accumulated mucus and catarrh, and is sometimes used by herbalists to help alleviate sinusitis.

The time of cold, damp weather brings us to several more of ginger's long-treasured benefits. It is plainly a warming remedy and many a cold and chill has been warded off by people who have accidentally become "chilled to the bone" or "soaked to the skin" - in two oft-repeated and traditionally British expressions   by drinking a cup of hot ginger tea at the earliest opportunity. It is also a comfort for those suffering from influenza, bronchitis and coughs, according to Chinese doctors who regard these ailments as signs of invading cold and damp. Gargling with ginger tea has also been used as a remedy to soothe sore throats.

Ginger has long been known to have a stimulating effect on the circulation.

The cold weather can bring with it other health problems - that of poor circulation because, as capillaries or small arteries constrict, blood flow is impeded resulting in cold and bluish-looking extremities such as fingers and toes, and the added distress of chilblains. The elderly, particularly, tend to suffer from poor circulation, as well as those who are generally run-down and worn-out.

The good news here is that hot and spicy herbs like ginger have long been known to have a stimulating effect on the circulation - that is why you can feel them warming you up, as the blood flows faster and moves nearer to the skin's surface. As well as helping the body to build up its defence system, this also has a generally tonic effect - and all this may well be the reasoning behind ginger's supposed aphrodisiac effect of historical note!

Fresh ginger or ginger pickle is always served with raw fish and other seafood dishes in Japanese cuisine.

Apart from taking ginger internally, herbalists often suggest a ginger bath to help improve circulation. This is also said to be particularly beneficial for people suffering from rheumatic or arthritic joint pains, as well as sore and stiff muscles.

As well as being particularly prone to suffering from circulatory problems, the elderly may experience loss of appetite with the added danger of not taking in enough nutrients to cope with their extra needs, and lack of secretion of gastric juices with resulting in poor digestion. Here, again, ginger comes to the rescue and can be taken in drinks by adding a good pinch of dried ginger to any suitable hot beverage, or a little crystallised or raw ginger root can be nibbled on to good effect.

Another suggestion to help soothe, warm and comfort sore and stiff areas of the body is to wring out a cloth in that good old standby, hot ginger tea, and apply it where it hurts. Aromatherapists may suggest using oil of ginger heavily diluted in a base of sesame oil (overdoing it will irritate the skin), adding just a drop to a favourite blend especially of citrus oils, or combined with rosemary and coriander to massage into rheumaticky hands and feet to help increase the flow of blood to these areas.

And both the very young and very old may experience occasional attacks of diarrhoea, for which a little ginger may just provide the answer. In fact, it is used for this purpose in several parts of the world, just at it is for food poisoning, for which it can be a very effective remedy, especially when the cause of the problem is seafood. You may have noticed that fresh ginger or ginger pickle is always served with raw fish and other seafood dishes in Japanese cuisine and there is a very good reason for this!

In addition to its other revered attributes, ginger is used in Ayurvedic and Tibb systems of medicine to relieve nervous problems, gingivitis, toothache, painful menstruation and constipation. Ginger truly deserves its rapidly increasing popularity and, when we look at more scientifically based evidence of its virtues, not only are there confirmed cases, but we shall also see that proof of ginger's efficacy in other areas is starting to come to light.

GINGER COMPRESS: *Wring out a cloth in strong, hot ginger tea and apply to the affected area. Helpful for sore and painful muscles and joints, and for sprains and swelling.*

GINGER TEA: *13 - 25g/¹/₂ - 1oz grated or minced fresh, thinly-peeled (a lot of the goodness lies just under the skin) ginger root, or up to 2 tsp ginger powder. 575ml/1pt boiling water*
Pour boiling water over the ginger, stir, and leave to stand, covered, for 5 - 10 minutes or until cool enough to drink. Strain if necessary and drink a small cupful before or after meals or when required. You can also add a good pinch of ground ginger to any hot drink for a speedy way to experience its benefits.
This is especially useful for digestive problems and flatulence, and a hot cupful also helps to ward off colds and chills, and speed up the circulation. Gargle with it if you have a sore throat, or add a little honey and sip to soothe a cough.

GINGER BATH: *5cm/1 inch piece of fresh ginger root, grated or finely chopped or from 1sp to 1tbsp ground ginger. 1 litre/4 cups water*
Stir together and simmer until the liquid turns yellow if using the root, or the powder has dissolved. Strain if necessary and swirl into a bath of very warm water. Useful for sore and aching joints and muscles, to speed up circulation or stop a cold in its tracks.

CHAPTER 4

A HOT FUTURE FOR GINGER

Nowadays, scientific interest in the properties of a number of plants, already used and trusted by millions of people around the world, is steadily rising as chemical analysis and biological investigation is confirming traditionally respected benefits. Ginger, in particular, is gaining increasing respect as more and more of its long-revered potential attributes are acquiring scientific backing.

So what exactly is the basis for its growing popularity? Ginger is a very complex substance. It has a reasonable level of protein - something approaching 9 % - also fats and starch, a noticeable content of vitamin A and niacin, and minerals such as calcium and iron, plus amino acids. However, the main interest in its beneficial effects is centred on the actions of its essential oil which is made up of more than 200 chemical components, and the oleoresin which is a thick oily paste extracted from the rhizome, the principle constituents of which are substances called gingerols.

long-revered potential attributes are acquiring scientific backing.

Over the last decade several studies have confirmed these traditional claims.

The oleoresin also contains other active ingredients, most importantly shogaol and zingerone. Recently, it has been discovered that shogaols - a breakdown product of gingerols, produced only after drying - are twice as pungent as gingerols.

The distinctive aroma and taste of ginger comes from its pungent yellow oil with its content of sweet and spicy zingerone, and several tartly-flavoured chemicals including pepper-scented borneol, eucalyptol, and citral, with its lemon-like smell.

It is obviously important, when using ginger as a supplement for its health benefits, that its pungent components retain their potency and are of a consistent quality for maximum effect. To this end, ginger is now available in the form of capsules containing a standardised natural concentrated extract from the oleoresin.

Today, ginger is probably still best recognised by people as a useful anti-emetic, taken as a natural way to prevent travel sickness in particular, and feelings of nausea generally.

And over the last decade or so, several studies have confirmed these traditional claims. With regard to motion sickness, a much-quoted study in America by Daniel Mowrey and Dennis Clayson was published in *The Lancet* in 1982, and described the varying effects of ginger capsules (totalling 940mg), an anti-histamine used in a popular anti-travel sickness product, and a placebo, on 36 undergraduates who had reported a particularly high susceptibility to motion sickness.

The volunteers were blindfolded and placed in a tilted revolving chair for up to six minutes to induce motion sickness. None of the subjects who had taken the placebo or anti-histamine was able to stay in the chair for the allotted time, whilst half of those who had taken the ginger lasted the full session.

Another trial which reported positive effects for ginger involved a group of 80 Danish naval cadets on board a training ship in late 1985. None of the cadets was used to sailing in high seas, or known to be particularly susceptible to motion sickness, and half the group was given 1 gram of powdered ginger root, while the rest took a placebo of identical appearance. The result was that the ginger root was found to be significantly better than the placebo in reducing frequency of vomiting and cold sweats.

Another trial which reported positive effects for ginger involved a group of 80 Danish naval cadets on board a training ship in late 1985.

This is good news for those who suffer from travel sickness and wish to avoid the possible problems of drowsiness and blurred vision which accompany some over-the-counter drug-based remedies, as ginger has no reported side-effects.

These findings led another group of researchers in Britain to consider that a preparation of ginger root might reduce nausea after an operation (when it can be a common and distressing after-effect of anaesthesia), as they reasoned that the aromatic and carminative properties of ginger might block gastrointestinal reactions and subsequent nausea feedback.

Factors known to provoke post-operative nausea and vomiting were taken into consideration and the effect of capsules prepared from ginger, a standard antiemetic, and a placebo was compared on a group of 60 women who had undergone major gynaecological surgery. Statistically, there was found to be significantly fewer cases of nausea in those who had taken ginger root compared with the placebo, and the number of cases of nausea in the groups who took ginger root or the standard antiemetic was similar.

In India ginger is frequently added to a diet rich in fat.

Nausea and vomiting are also debilitating side-effects for patients receiving cytotoxic drugs (used to destroy cancer cells in chemotherapy). Research led by Johji Yamahara at Kyoto Pharmaceutical University in Japan, and published in 1989, indicated that ginger had anti-vomiting action and that its effectiveness was comparable to an standard antiemetic drug - in fact, both substances totally prevented vomiting.

In 1990, a study was carried out in Denmark on 27 pregnant women who suffered from morning sickness. Again, the results were positive, with 19 of the women finding that ginger had reduced the degree of nausea and number of vomiting attacks. The amount of ginger used was similar to that found in ginger-flavoured food and drink.

Ginger boasts a number of other interesting effects which are constantly being confirmed. For example, in India ginger is frequently added to a diet rich in fat, and the reasoning behind this, whether instinctive or not, is now becoming apparent.

A HOT FUTURE FOR GINGER

Professor K C Srivastava at Odense University's Institute of Community Health in Denmark, has reported that ginger can inhibit blood clotting even more efficiently than garlic or onion, which are already well-known for this effect, and results increase in relation to the amount used. This is an effect also noticed by other researchers, including Dr Charles Dorso of Cornell University Medical College. He and his colleagues believe ginger's blood-thinning compound to be gingerol, which has a similar chemical structure to aspirin, also known for its anti-clotting ability.

Diets with a high fat content contribute to the increasing incidence of atherosclerosis and coronary heart disease, so the balancing addition of ginger, garlic, and other such ingredients to high fat diet, along with ginger or a placebo. The addition of ginger had a significantly beneficial effect and led the researchers to state: "As there is sufficient evidence supporting the involvement of platelets in the genesis and development of atherosclerosis, administration of natural products like ginger may prove beneficial in thromboatherosclerosis".

long-revered potential attributes are acquiring scientific backing.

There have also been studies by Japanese researchers which show that ginger can have a tonic effect on the heart and may help to lower blood pressure, as well as helping to lower cholesterol levels by reducing its absorption in the blood and liver. This latter effect has been confirmed in tests on rats by Indian researchers.

Even more recently, and with great excitement, ginger has been identified by medical researchers Professor K C Srivastava and Dr Tariq Mustafa, at Odense University in Denmark, as a particularly safe and effective remedy for the pain and swelling suffered by victims of arthritis and rheumatism.

The results of taking ginger for patients with osteoarthritis were astonishing.

They studied the effects of ginger in relieving the pain and swelling suffered by a group of patients afflicted by rheumatoid arthritis and osteoarthritis, and came up with very interesting and important results. Well over half the patients who took ginger regularly noted a "marked" relief from symptoms, and of the remainder about half again experienced either "moderate" or "minimal" relief.

Ginger's effectiveness in controlling both pain and swelling varied according to whether it was used to relieve symptoms of rheumatoid arthritis or osteoarthritis. For example, 74% of those suffering from rheumatoid arthritis noted "marked" pain relief, with "moderate" relief experienced by another 11%. With regard to reduction in the swelling caused by rheumatoid arthritis, 59% enjoyed "marked" relief, with a further 18% noting a "moderate" improvement.

The results of taking ginger for patients with osteoarthritis were also astonishing, with 55% reporting a "marked" improvement in the degree of pain suffered, and other 22% experiencing "moderate" improvement. Exactly half the patients noted a marked improvement in the swelling associated with osteoarthritis, and 20% a moderate improvement.

These excellent results show that ginger is just as effective, and often better, than modern drugs used to control symptoms of arthritic disease, and it offers the inestimable additional benefit of avoiding their side-effects, which can include severe stomach upsets or gastro-intestinal bleeding.

It is not yet quite understood exactly why ginger is so effective but Dr Mustafa said: "We think that ginger inhibits two of the enzymes that cause arthritic pain". He also thought it likely that ginger brought about the improvements by "interfering with the production and release of products of lipid membranes, peptides and proteins, and amino acids".

The amount of ginger used in the Danish study ranged between 1 and 2 grams daily ($^1/_2$ - 1 teaspoonful), and improvements experienced by patients were maintained as long as they kept taking the ginger. Many of those who stopped taking ginger daily suffered a recurrence of symptoms within a few weeks but regained the same degree of pain and swelling relief after resuming the ginger therapy.

Results show that ginger is just as effective, and often better, than modern drugs.

The huge importance of these results is highlighted by the fact that an estimated 20 million people in Britain today are affected by rheumatism and arthritis, which are the biggest single cause of severe disability in this country and account for the loss or more than 80 million working days every year.

There is no doubt that we shall be hearing much more about ginger's excellent
potential health benefits in the future. Research is already being undertaken
into its ability to prevent and relieve headaches and migraine; it is known to
have potent antioxidant activity; and there is much interest in its ability to
improve, or should we say "ginger up" blood circulation.

So whether you choose to take ginger as a supplement in standardised
capsule form for a particular health purpose, eat or drink it with meals and
enjoy its distinctive spicy flavour and warming effects, bathe in it or use the
oil to massage with, or the tea to soak a compress in, there are any one of
a wealth of ways to enjoy ginger's many benefits - some of which we don't
yet even know but are sure to be hearing about very soon

long-revered
potential
attributes are
acquiring
scientific
backing.

GROWING YOUR OWN GINGER

Ginger (*Zingiber officinalis*) is a member of the Zingiberaceae family, and the name zingiber derives from a Sanskrit word which means horn or antler shaped, referring to the shape of the rhizome from which it grows.

Probably native to South-East Asia, ginger is now grown commercially throughout the tropics and many types and grades are available. These days, ginger may come from Australia, India, China, Jamaica, Fiji, Central America, Nigeria, Sierra Leone, Brazil, Thailand and a number of Caribbean Islands.

The name zingiber derives from a Sanskrit word which means horn or antler shaped.

GROWING YOUR OWN GINGER

Ginger is a perennial tuberous rhizome which creeps horizontally and increases underground. A reed or cane like green stem grows from the rhizome annually in the Spring up to a maximum height of about one metre, and the lance-shaped leaves are 1 - 2cm wide and 15 - 30cm long. The flowers are a pale yellowish colour with a purple lip and have an aromatic smell.

Ideally, ginger likes a hot, humid and shady place in which to grow with a temperature of at least 24°/75F. Many of its wild relatives can still be found growing as part of the ground flora of tropical lowland forests and this is probably where its own origins lie. However, it is possible to grow it in this country in a conservatory or greenhouse, and some enthusiastic gardeners have succeeded in keeping it in a pot on a warm patio through the summer months.

Some enthusiastic gardeners have succeeded in keeping it in a pot on a warm patio through the summer months.

Plant pieces of fresh rhizome early in the year (ginger needs a 10 month growing season for optimum rhizome production) in well-drained, nutrient-rich peaty compost in a warm, humid place. Keep the compost moist until the first shoot appears and keep the plants well watered when they start to grow vigorously. Ginger makes an elegant and unusual foliage plant and a decorative addition to the conservatory or patio.

Reduce watering as the leaves start to die down towards the end of the year. When the leaves have dried out, dig up the rootstock and remove remains of stem and root fibres, wash thoroughly, and allow the rhizomes to dry out, ideally in the sun. Young fresh rhizomes will last for 2- 3 months in a cool, dry place.

These young fresh rhizomes, also called green ginger, are used for cooking, and can also be soaked in brine and vinegar before processing in sugar syrups of increasing strengths until they are suitable for use as the product called crystallised or candied ginger. The part of the rhizome closest to the stem is known as stem ginger and has a more delicate flavour - it is often preserved in a heavy syrup and widely used in sweet dishes.

The part of the rhizome closest to the stem is known as stem ginger - it is often preserved in a heavy syrup.

Mature rhizomes are peeled (and are then known as "white ginger") and usually ground into powder for various uses.
Oil is distilled from unpeeled, dried and ground rhizomes.

Like most roots, fresh ginger should be very thinly peeled for use as all the richest oils and resins lie just beneath the skin.

CHAPTER 6

COOKING
WITH GINGER

In countries around the world, people have been enjoying the taste of ginger in all kinds of recipes for many centuries. Indeed, in China and India, ginger plays an integral part in a whole host of savoury main meal dishes.

Nowadays, we tend to associate ginger more with confectionery, cakes and biscuits, and drinks - as in crystallised ginger, gingerbread, parkin, ginger biscuits, ginger snaps, ginger wine, ginger ale, ginger beer, and so on - but it can add a spicy kick to all manner of dishes, as the following recipes will show. All recipes serve four.

White Stilton & Ginger Pate *(above)*

Carrot & Ginger Soup *(below)*

CARROT AND GINGER SOUP

500g/1lb carrots, thinly sliced
50g/2oz butter
900ml/1 1/2 pints vegetable stock
5fl oz cultured buttermilk
5cm/2 inch piece of fresh ginger,
peeled and grated
or finely chopped
sea salt
freshly ground black pepper

Sauté carrots and ginger in half the butter in a large saucepan for about 10 minutes. Stir in the stock and cook until the carrots are soft. Allow to cool a little then blend or purée and return to the saucepan to reheat, stirring in the remaining butter and salt and pepper to taste. When warmed through, swirl in the buttermilk - do not allow to boil. Serve immediately, decorated with chopped parsley.

WHITE STILTON AND GINGER PATE

350g/12oz white stilton
75/3oz butter
1 tbsp dry sherry
1 dsp very finely chopped
stem ginger
1/2 tsp mustard powder

Crumble and mash cheese in a mixing bowl. Melt the butter and stir two-thirds into the cheese, together with the sherry, ginger and mustard powder. The mixture should now be quite smooth and creamy. Divide between four small ramekin dishes and pour remaining butter over the top. Refrigerate for at least two hours to allow the paté to set.
Serve with salad and wholemeal bread.

Chinese Chop Suey *(above)*

Pineapple, Kiwi & Ginger Cocktail *(below)*

PINEAPPLE, KIWI & GINGER COCKTAIL

1 large ripe pineapple
3 large kiwis
juice of one large orange
grated rind of one orange
1 heaped dsp. finely chopped
or minced stem ginger
1 tbsp orange liqueur (optional)

Peel, core and slice the pineapple, then cut the slices into slivers. Peel and thinly slice the kiwis, then halve the slices. Divide the fruit between four glass serving dishes. Stir the ginger into the orange juice, and add liqueur if liked, then pour over the fruit. Decorate with a sprig of mint and chill until required Sprinkle on the orange rind when complete.

CHINESE CHOP SUEY

250g fresh bean sprouts
100g button mushrooms (chunks)
100g mixed red/green/orange peppers (finely sliced)
50g fresh broccoli florets (small)
1 lge. sliced celery stalk
2 lge. ripe tomatoes (small pieces)
3-4 med. shallots (finely chopped)
2 cloves garlic (crushed)
1 inch raw ginger (cut as julienne)
Soy sauce
Oyster sauce
Sesame seed oil
Corn or sunflower oil
Plain flour
Black pepper and sea salt
Ensure vegetables are not too wet.

Heat 2 tbsps vegetable oil with 1 tsp Sesame oil in large pan until they start to simmer. Add shallots, garlic & ginger. When shallots lightly brown, add 1 tsp Oyster sauce & 1 tsp Soy sauce. Stir well. Quickly add broccoli & mushrooms. Heat rapidly. When mushrooms begin to sweat, transfer mix to a warm dish. Add peppers & celery to remaining liquid (use a little more vegetable oil if needed) & fry for about 4 mins. Add bean sprouts & tomato & fry for further 2 mins always stirring. Remove from heat. Mix 2 level tsp plain flour in 5 tbsps cold water - ensure no lumps. Add to pan. Stir for 2 mins then add shallot, mushroom & broccoli mix & cook for 2 mins. Taste & season.

Roasted Vegetables with Ginger *(above)*

Cod and Prawns in a Lemon & Ginger Sauce *(below)*

ROASTED VEGETABLES WITH GINGER

6 tbsp extra virgin olive oil

1 small aubergine, sliced

2 courgettes, sliced lengthwise

1 large red onion, thinly sliced

4 large tomatoes, sliced

1 large yellow pepper, deseeded and quartered

1 large red pepper, deseeded and quartered

2 x 5cm/2 inch pieces of fresh ginger root, peeled and grated

Brush one or two large baking sheets with oil and spread the sliced vegetables out over these. Brush well with remaining oil and scatter the grated ginger over the vegetables. Roast near top of oven at 200℃/400F/gas mark 6 for 30 to 45 minutes until softened and brown at the edges.

This makes a tasty supper served with garlic focaccia or you can layer it with cooked pasta penne or rigatoni, top with grated mozzarella and bake for 20 to 25 minutes on 180℃/350F/gas mark 4 for a filling main meal.

COD AND PRAWNS IN A LEMON & GINGER SAUCE

750g/1 1/2lb cod fillet

100g/4oz cooked prawns

Juice and a little finely grated rind of one lemon

150m l5/fl oz milk

150/5 fl oz vegetable stock

25g/1oz butter

25g/1oz flour

5cm/2 inch piece of fresh ginger root, peeled and grated

1 good tsp brown sugar

sea salt

freshly ground black pepper

Bake the cod in a little milk at 180℃/350F/gas mark 4 for 15 - 20 minutes. Meanwhile, melt butter in saucepan, add ginger and lemon rind, cook for one minute, stir in flour and cook for one or two minutes. Slowly add milk and stock, stirring all the time, and bring to the boil. Add lemon juice, sugar and salt and pepper to taste, then stir in prawns. Remove cod from oven, transfer to warmed serving dish, and pour the lemon and ginger sauce over.

Serve at once with broccoli florets and sautéed potatoes.

Chicken Stir-fry with Ginger *(above)*

Pork with Apple in a Butter & Ginger Sauce *(below)*

PORK WITH APPLE IN A BUTTER & GINGER SAUCE

750g/1 ½ lb pork fillet

1 lge cooking apple, peeled, cored and thickly sliced

a little vegetable oil

75g/3oz butter

5cm/2 inch piece of fresh ginger root, peeled and grated

Slice pork fillet fairly thinly (1cm/¼ inch) and fry in a large pan in a little vegetable oil until it starts to brown. Add ginger and apple slices and cook gently for five more minutes or until apple starts to soften very slightly. Add butter and stir in until melted - do not allow to burn. Remove pork and apple slices to a warmed serving dish and pour over the melted butter and ginger.

Serve with baby new potatoes, baby carrots and mange tout.

CHICKEN STIR FRY WITH GINGER

2 boned chicken breasts, cut into thin strips

250g/8oz bean sprouts

2 courgettes, very thinly sliced

1 lge carrot, scrubbed and julienned

1 lge green pepper, deseeded and cut into thin strips

1 lge red pepper, deseeded and cut into thin strips

1 lge onion, finely chopped

3 sticks green celery, finely sliced

2 cloves garlic, peeled and finely chopped or minced

5cm/2 inch piece of fresh ginger root, peeled and grated

2 tbsp vegetable or nut oil

2 tbsp dry sherry

1 dsp soy sauce

In a wok or large, heavy-bottomed frying-pan sauté chicken, onion and celery in the oil for a few minutes, then add ginger and garlic and stir well. Add peppers, carrot and courgette and stir on a high heat until they start to soften, then add the bean sprouts. Finally, stir in sherry and soy sauce and cook for a few more minutes.

Serve at once with rice or Chinese noodles.

Gingerbread *(above)*

Rhubarb & Ginger Brown Betty *(below)*

RHUBARB & GINGER BROWN BETTY

50g/1lb rhubarb, washed and cut into 5cm/2 inch chunks

250g/8oz wholewheat breadcrumbs

50g/2oz butter, melted

1 heaped tbsp demerara sugar

1 good tsp ground ginger

1 tbsp finely chopped stem ginger

1 tbsp honey

juice of an orange

Place rhubarb in an ovenproof dish. Mix together stem ginger, honey and orange juice and pour over the rhubarb. Stir the melted butter into the breadcrumbs, add sugar and ground ginger and mix well. Spread evenly over the rhubarb. Bake on the middle shelf of the oven at 180ᶜ/350F/gas mark 4 for 30 to 40 minutes.

GINGERBREAD

125g/4oz butter

3 tbsp molasses

3 tbsp golden syrup

150ml/5fl oz milk

2 med eggs

250g/8oz wholemeal self-raising flour

1/2 tsp ground ginger

1/2 tsp bicarbonate of soda

Grease and line a 20cm/8 inch square cake tin. Melt together the butter molasses, golden syrup and milk. Leave to cool. Mix flour, ginger and bicarbonate of soda in a mixing bowl. Beat the eggs and stir into the flour mix, then stir in the melted ingredients and beat together well. Pour into prepared cake tin and bake for about one hour at 180ᶜ/350F/gas mark 4 on the middle shelf of the oven.

Chocolate Mascarpone & Ginger Cheesecake
(above)

Ginger, Honey & Choc-chip Ice Cream
(below)

GINGER, HONEY & CHOC-CHIP ICE CREAM

300ml/ $^1/_2$ pint double cream

2 tbsp milk

2 tbsp honey

1 good dsp finely chopped
stem ginger

1 dsp ginger syrup

50g/2oz plain chocolate chips

Beat cream and milk together until just stiff. Stir in the honey. Pour into a shallow tray and freeze for at least 30 to 40 minutes or until the mixture is starting to set round the edge of the tray. Remove from freezer, turn into bowl, beat until smooth, add ginger and choc chips and stir in well. Return to tray and freeze.

Serve with ginger snaps.

CHOCOLATE MASCARPONE & GINGER CHEESECAKE

500g/1lb mascarpone cheese

250g/8oz good quality
plain chocolate

1 tbsp finely chopped
stem ginger

1 dsp ginger syrup

250g/8oz ginger biscuits,
crushed

50g/2oz melted butter

Stir melted butter into crushed biscuits and press firmly into base of greased, loose-bottomed 20cm/8 inch cake tin. Melt chocolate into a bowl over a saucepan of boiling water. Beat mascarpone until smooth and mix in the melted chocolate gradually. Stir in the chopped ginger and syrup and spoon the mixture onto the biscuit base. Put in fridge to set for an hour or two, then remove from tin and decorate and grated white chocolate. Sprinkle with Cocoa powder when complete.

INDEX

GINGER